A MANAGEMENT BY OBJECTIVES

OKR and BPM TOGETHER IN PRACTICE

Strategic Management of your Business Processes.

This version was published on 2024-06-13.

© Cláudio Pires

Contents

A MANAGEMENT BY OBJECTIVES 1

DEDICATION 2

MISSION 3

VISION 4

IN PRACTICE 5

PART I A MANAGEMENT BY OBJECTIVES 7

The invitation to A Management By Objectives 8

Understanding of a Management By Objectives 12

An Integrated Management By Objectives 20

PART II THE HEART OF THE STRATEGY 32

Why? 33

Commitment to Mission and Vision 34

More Objective Examples 37

PART III THE BRAIN OF TACTICS 39

How? 40

Project Planning	42
The Key Results	51
PART IV THE BODY IN ACTION	54
O quê?	55
Business Process Management	56
The Initiatives	59
Examples of Initiatives	61
PART V INTEGRATED COORDINATION	64
When?	65
Measurement and Communication	68
The success	80
PART VI A NEW VISION	82
Innovation	83
Culture	85
A Life for Goals	89
WHAT LEFT TO BE SAID?	91
About me and where we meet	92
About my books and the Management in Practice series	95

DEDICATION

"I arrived in time to see you wake up. I came running ahead of the Sun. I opened the door and, before entering, I reviewed my entire life... I thought of everything that is possible to talk about (that are only good for the two of us): signs of good, vital desires, small fragments of light. To talk about the color of the storms, the blue sky, the April flowers; to think beyond good and evil, to remember things that no one has seen. The world is there, always spinning, and, on top of it, everything goes: who knows, that means love! Road to make the dream come true..."–Milton Nascimento, "Who Knows This Means Love" ("Quem Sabe Isso Quer Dizer Amor" in Portuguese).

"Little girl, how cute you are: a little one like that, starting to live. Stay like this, my love, without growing; because the world is bad. It's bad and you will suddenly suffer disappointment; because life alone is your bogeyman. Stay like this, stay like this, always like this; and remember me, for the things that I have given you. And don't forget me either, when you finally know everything I kept."–Toquinho, "Waltz for a Little Girl" ("Valsa Para Uma Menininha" in Portuguese).

MISSION

I write about everything I wish someone had already written and that I also missed reading. I only communicate about what I have already lived, experienced, learned, made mistakes and needed to organize in my head, for a better professional performance. I write and communicate with theory and practice, balancing the simple and the complex, for a better business world. May my books also promote your career, your job, your team, your work sector and your company.

VISION

I seek to establish a career as an author of business books, accompanied by offering training, lectures, consultancy and mentoring; through extensive proprietary content, recognized innovative performance, continuous creative solutions and a real delivery of value to those who reserve their time and attention. The proposal is for all of us to follow an executive path of leadership, reputation and better business results; in renewed partnership and trust. One day, I intend to be your favorite author.

IN PRACTICE

Do! They will criticize you anyway... The world already has too many people seeking profit; The world needs more people looking for quality. In whatever you do, do the best you can. And do it every day. Be aware of what you represent. Seek the truth that unites theory and practice. Postpone your recognition. Trust the path. Always communicate as you would with a friend. Understand your pains, but leave them in the past. Master your words and encourage your actions. Read and reread. Do it and redo it. Repeat many times! So learn from what you did: feel justifiably proud. Take the opportunity to review your process once again. Focus on what you are doing again, right now. Be aware! Organize your ideas. Move slowly, but always move forward. Keep it up, for 1 month, 1 year, 10 years, 1 lifetime. Turn your scars into creative use. Know why you do it. Do what has to be done; when it has to be done. Do a little more and don't stop. Boil your head! (laughs) Write the first sentence and believe it. Write as many sentences as possible. Follow the writing flow. The competition is internal, with ourselves. Develop your technique; study what you need. Nothing more! Know when to get straight to the point and when to introduce a new concept. Be agile, but don't be hasty. Trust your memory and the intelligence of your trajectory. Follow the path that takes best care of you. Transform resistance into collaboration. When everything goes wrong, you can still turn to art (we will always have Paul McCartney songs)... Challenge limits, be kind and bring together partners. Work not to become the best professional, but to be a better person; your best version! Develop your work to the state of the art, deeply. Receive criticism just like you receive praise. If you know how to do it, you will show your experience. Exclude unnecessary behaviors. Show your personal touch. Work without fear. Recognize new truths when you hear them. Carry on.

When you go further, continue a little longer. Don't stop changing. Accept the imperfections of preliminary versions. Deliver, without worrying about getting it back. But receive it with gratitude! Don't worry so much about those who don't want to be helped. Read those who have written before you. Encourage those who come next. Get out of the "box", the limiting way. Wake up, you are ready: forget all the rules and improvise. Again: forget all the rules and improvise!

PART I A MANAGEMENT BY OBJECTIVES

The invitation to A Management By Objectives

"You got a fast car. I want a ticket to anywhere. Maybe, we make a deal. Maybe, together, we can get somewhere. Any place is better. Starting from zero, got nothing to loose. Maybe we'll make something. Me, myself, I got nothing to prove."–Tracy Chapman, "Fast Car"

Follow my cordial call. Pack your bags for an important mission to accomplish. Trials ahead, the prize will be guaranteed professional and personal discovery. I will help you decide what really needs to be done. Mitigating crises and dangers, the proposal is a trajectory of change and transformation, throughout this reading: an inspiring "Hero's Journey"[1].

* * *

Volatility, **uncertainty**, **complexity** e **ambiguity**: yes, we will only survive if we know how to be a little crazier, in this complex "V.U.C.A. World"[2]

Everything around us is very fast: science, technology and business; and everything is also very unpredictable.

But calm down, breathe...

---
[1] https://en.wikipedia.org/wiki/Hero%27s_journey
[2] https://en.wikipedia.org/wiki/VUCA

There is a solution! And the solution is in the flexible agility[3]: it's about better knowing how to lean, deflect or twist; accept and "embrace" the inevitable changes, developing a calm and superior capacity for decision-making and prioritization.

- For more **collaboration**.
- For more **resultados**.
- For more **adaptation**.
- For more **experimentation**.

Hmm, it makes sense; and that's what we're here for!

*   *   *

Mission, **Vision** and **Principles**, in transparent alignment of the **strategy** (from point A to point B); as set out in my initial personal presentation.

- **Why?**
- **How?**
- **What?**

So, in the next sections, you will evolve through this division above, into its main parts.

Each part aims to make reading and reasoning easier, composing the mental model of this book, so that you:

- feel stimulated by the **opportunity** of the topic,
- understand how to carry out your implementation **project**,
- keep such **service** "alive" and
- go a little further, in creativity and **innovation**.

---
[3] https://agilemanifesto.org/

To be more specific, we want to:

- understand very well what "OKRs" represent,
- design a process for implementing "OKRs",
- manage the execution of this implemented process,
- Customize and extend the default process without fear.

I want to bring you answers to the same questions I have asked myself in the past, to truly understand the purpose of **a management by objectives**:

- What do we want to achieve with any set of OKRs?
- What risks and opportunities should be considered when defining such OKRs?
- How to balance realistic but challenging objectives to drive and demonstrate growth?
- How to measure progress towards goals?
- How to align vision and strategy across all teams, across the entire organization?
- What resources, support and collaborations are needed?
- What is the expected pace and what ceremonies are suggested, in adherence to the standard process?
- What actions or initiatives need to be carried out?
- How to follow, guide and record learning?
- How to celebrate successes and overcome challenges along the way?

Therefore, I believe in the complete book: in its title, in its didactic orientation and in the success of each reader; without prolonged introductions, with a concrete practical demonstration of the concepts and highlighting the author's experience.

"Straight to the point" and without sounding like a historical dissertation: because, after all, it is a business book, business-oriented.

From these first lines, I just want you to follow without anxiety, in pleasant comfort and confident guidance: that you feel guided, experience real experiences, prepare your own reflections, be confident in the learning you have achieved and know how to plan your next actions, in a great read.

Understanding of a Management By Objectives

"Well, now, I'm no hero: that's understood. All the redemption I can offer, girl, is beneath this dirty hood. With a chance to make it good somehow, hey, what else can we do now? Except, roll down the window and let the wind blow back your hair. Well, the night's busting open and these two lanes will take us anywhere. We got one last chance to make it real. To trade in these wings on some wheels. Climb in back. Heaven's waiting on down the tracks." – Bruce Springsteen, "Thunder Road"

Think about "alignment." All together, in collaboration, adding efforts. No distractions, no hypes, no doubts about what is a priority. With focus and clarity. Daily. Monthly. Annually. A **total alignment**.

Unbeatable, right?!

So, this is the objective of any leadership and the objective of **a management by objectives**:

- manage limited resources,
- to optimize the delivery of results,
- that really matter.

It's worth emphasizing this phrase a little more...

Resources are clearly limited (time, energy, money) and will run out anyway: with or without management over them. Accept, too, that optimal deliveries are actually quite different from reasonable or just-enough deliveries. And there is no point in delivering something very good without its practical application.

Yes, it is complex: it involves rhythm, it involves discipline, it seeks to be sustainable and agile, without waste (of time, people, material, money), in continuous adaptation and improvement, in favor of excellence and happiness.

Because **happiness** will always be the purpose of all good management! ;-)

At the end of the day, it is pleasant to return home with the justified pride of absolute, unquestionable progress.

Thus, we could classify our theme as "management by guidelines".

Or, if you prefer another existing term, "administration by objectives".

Nowadays, however, it is more common to use the acronym, "OKR" (*"Objectives and Key Results"*).

In the past, it was all about "organizational measurement."

I prefer to call, in my work, "**A** Management By Objectives" (with emphasis on this undefined article, which makes up the title of the book): after all, it is not the only one, it is another one, it is my interpretation; which seeks to attract and embrace all these similarities mentioned in the terms above.

"A Management By Objectives" = "Management By Guidelines" + "Administration By Objectives" + "OKRs" + "Organizational Measurement"

I'm not concerned here with establishing the differences: I'm more interested in the strength of the whole, the total of that sum!

And, as already explained, all happiness needs this degree of freedom, creativity and a certain revolution: I think I also heard you saying that you would like to change the world, right?!

Rigid paths (whether processes or books), full of rules and restrictions, tend to be boring, tedious and threatening. Accept this lighter idea, with confidence in the author and transparency of the content. In the end, also customize your own implementation!

*   *   *

Even though it is "**A Management By Objectives**", we will not fail to know what the classical approach preaches, what drives the common use of the standard process.

Google, Spotify, Twitter, LinkedIn, AirBnB, Amazon, Adobe, Uber, Dropbox, Oracle; to name just a few of the big adopters of OKRs.

But how did we get here?

Standing on the shoulders of giants!

Yes, out of great respect and admiration, it is worth, now, a minimum historical reference...

We started with the original implementation of the Management By Objectives, in **1954**, with the extraordinary **Peter Drucker**[1], in his book "The Practice Of Management"[2]: there was the foundation of balance and harmony between the personal objectives of employees and the strategic objectives of the organization.

Even if it's still a little more focused on the "what?" than in the "how?", strongly hierarchical in silos/sectors and top management, a little shy in confronting risks and with long annual review and update intervals, Drucker's approach disseminated a lot, a lot of inspiration.

It is likely that this approach still persists today in some company you know: an outdated, but admirable, longevity.

In a second highlight, we then had **Andrew Grove**[3], the CEO who transformed Intel, from **1987** to 1998, and evolved Drucker's

---

[1] https://en.wikipedia.org/wiki/Peter_Drucker
[2] https://www.amazon.com/Practice-Management-Peter-F-Drucker/dp/0060878975
[3] https://en.wikipedia.org/wiki/Andrew_Grove

idealization into two simple and fundamental questions: "where do I want to get to?" and "how will I know if I'm getting there?"; creating the modern OKRs (*"Objectives and Key Results"*) model.

"Andy" Grove incorporated changes to Drucker's model, adopting a more frequent evaluation of results (monthly to quarterly) and seeking much more challenging and aggressive results, as he wrote in "High Output Management"[4].

From this personalized "iMBO" (*"Intel's Management By Objectives"*), Grove further extended its adaptation to a more public and transparent communication, of interests motivated by the "factory floor" and without fueling expectations for bonuses, rewards or financial compensation.

And, in a last stage of consolidation, we have **John Doerr**[5], president of Kleiner Perkins, an investment market company, who worked at Intel. He then disseminated the methodology to some companies in his portfolio, with the main emphasis on Google ("Measure What Matters: How Google, Bono, and the Gates Foundation Rock the World with OKRs"[6]).

With Doerr and Google, OKRs gained worldwide fame and are currently used as an important performance management tool in several companies... including mine, [Fonte Oncological Pathology](https://fontemd.com /) ("Fonte Patologia Oncológica" in Portuguese)!

The main names in this beautiful evolution are: Peter Drucker >> Andrew Grove >> John Doerr.

It's also worth watching Rick Klau's video on YouTube ("How Google sets goals"[7]), about Google's popular implementation of OKRs: with an impressive number of over 1 million views!

Obviously, I read and I was interested in all the references above;

---

[4] https://www.amazon.com/High-Output-Management-Andrew-Grove
[5] https://en.wikipedia.org/wiki/John_Doerr
[6] https://www.amazon.com/dp/0525536221
[7] https://www.youtube.com/watch?v=mJB83EZtAjc

but I remained careful to add my own ideas, in a habitual writing of around 100 pages, starting from a first blank sheet, with the certainty of what I lived, experienced and organized, going "straight to the point" and in a style of writing that always resembles a pleasant conversation with a friend.

When it comes to OKRs, we have a lot available for free, but, unfortunately, nothing more than brief translations of these originals, in inflexible interpretations and shallow analyses: I don't believe in any "copy and paste".

* * *

And since we're talking about the classic term "organizational measurement", it's worth, as soon as possible, understanding some original differences between "**KPIs**" (*"Key Performance Indicators"*) and "**OKRs**" (*" Objectives and Key Results"*).

- Key Indicators are part of the usual **Operations**, while Key Results are part of the differentiated **Strategy**.
- Key Indicators make up a Dashboard[8] of instrumentation, while Key Results assign **goals to the measures**.
- Key Indicators are used in the **long term** and inform **comfortable maintenance** that everything works well, while Key Results are redefined in the **short term** and challenge **ambitious goals**.
- Key Indicators seek people's **involvement**, while Key Results require people's **commitment** (as in the fable ["The Chicken and the Pig"](https://en.wikipedia. org/wiki/The_Chicken_and_the_Pig): the chicken is only involved in the new restaurant "Eggs and Ham", while the pig is actually committed).
- Key Indicators help **execute the business**, while Key Results serve to **transform the business**.

---
[8]https://en.wikipedia.org/wiki/Dashboard

- Key Indicators are props for **process activities**, while Key Results support the **customer experience**.
- Priority Key Indicators evolve into Key Results (as the "Borg" race[9] would say, in the fiction "Star Trek": "resistance is futile, you will be assimilated").

Only from this clear differentiation (rarely present in most texts about KPIs or OKRs), I do believe that we can reach an understanding of a management by objectives!

Yes, your car's dashboard will provide you with useful information on fuel capacity, average consumption, instantaneous speed, average speed, distance traveled, temperature and engine speed, closing doors and windows, etc.; but this is no guarantee that you will arrive at your appointment on time.

I can now guarantee you the basic concept of OKRs, below.

OKR is a collaborative structure and goal-setting methodology that helps organizations achieve their goals through measurable results.

A methodology to align organizational strategy with goals and people, offering focus, transparency, engagement and responsibility.

Please note: we are moving forward! ;-)

* * *

"So Say We All"?!

How to obtain this desired **"total alignment"**, already mentioned as a premise (strong requirement) of a management by objectives?

Forcing, from top to bottom, through hierarchical impositions, flowing through the company's organizational chart, becomes an innocent, naive vision: it may have worked in 1954, with Peter

---

[9]https://en.wikipedia.org/wiki/Borg

Drucker, but it no longer works, or at least it is not so efficient... and, if we are talking about results, we need to be efficient.

We also no longer believe in magic formulas, gurus or "coaches" for everyone. Hiring the best professionals, acquiring the best tools, leaving everyone free without any hassle doesn't solve it either: an idiot, with a tool or a good idea, is still an idiot (oh, the thoughts of the software engineer Grady Booch[10] represent me so much)... and "A Management By Objectives" is too good as an idea to be discredited.

So...

Have you ever watched the fictional miniseries "Battlestar Galactica"[11]?

From the 2003 remake, the figure of Admiral William Adama stands out, played by the actor Edward James Olmos[12]: despite being a fictional character, he is one of my greatest inspirations as a leader (one day, who knows, I'll write: "Management Lessons by William Adama"; laughs).

Believe me: to this day, I don't see a better answer to creating a culture of alignment!

It works like this, in the series: whenever an event, an incident or a problem is presented to the combat aircraft crew, everyone is respected in their doubts, but, once the questions are over, the unison chorus is repeated: *"So Say We All"*.

In other words, in an assertive understanding of each communication, without anything else to clarify, everyone comes together around the respective content, assimilated by the group.

A demonstration of evident cohesion, of a strong sense of a responsible and collaborative team, maintaining respect for individual ideas and the moment of dialogue.

---

[10]https://en.wikipedia.org/wiki/Grady_Booch
[11]https://en.wikipedia.org/wiki/Battlestar_Galactica
[12]https://en.wikipedia.org/wiki/Edward_James_Olmos

In our company, in our corporate Chat environment, we call this agreement "**Aware and Committed**":

- if someone read a message and answered nothing, we still don't know (we can't say) whether they are aware;
- if you registered to be aware, but with uncertainty, you are expected to comment on the post, seeking additional clarification;
- but, in the end, with everything clear and complete, it is desired to observe a collective sequence of "Aware and Committed" notes.

Noting "aware and committed" brings hierarchies closer together, transforms everyone into real collaborators for solutions, brings strength and harmony to the group; In short, you gain, daily and incrementally, total alignment!

Besides being really nice to follow the evolution of this entire unit under construction...

Try it: in your team, sector or company. It's a strong speech, far from being a joke or mockery: the company represents us and we are the company. We've been doing it this way for over 10 years: every day and in every record of our internal communication.

It is the "**captain's voice**" that echoes: a voice of command; which can, indeed, remain gentle, flexible and non-violent, but always being perceived as leadership communication.

As we wanted to demonstrate, we continue in practice!

An Integrated Management By Objectives

"Freedom's just another word for nothin' left to lose. Nothin', I mean nothin' hon' if it ain't free. Yeah, feelin' good was easy, Lord, when he sang the blues. Yeah, feelin' good was good enough for me. Good enough for me and my Bobby Mcgee." – Janis Joplin, "Me and Booby McGee"

Of the sections that formally occupy a traditional "Business Case" document, we can list:

- Executive Summary,
- Business Description,
- Operations and Processes,
- Risk analysis,
- Management Team,
- Marketing, Sales and Financial Information,
- Business Milestones.

We can consider that the previous chapter, "Understanding of a Management By Objectives", has already brought us our "Executive Summary".

Now, to complete our concept of *integrated management*, by objectives, we will talk about:

- "A Management By Objectives" and Strategy Management (as "Business Description"),

- "A Management By Objectives" and Management By Processes (about "Operations and Processes"),
- "A Management By Objectives" and Risk Management ("Risk Analysis"),
- "A Management By Objectives" and Management With People ("Management Team"),
- "A Management By Objectives" and Commercial and Financial Management ("Marketing, Sales and Financial Information").

What I want, here, is to "present you with this idea", my "*business case*": I have a proposed architecture for the solution and I intend for you to be my sponsor; I need to charm you, but I need to be brief and clear.

And that's exactly how our usual and busy corporate life works, right?!

Consolidating the initial success, we will move forward, evolving the next "Business Milestones"! ;-)

* * *

About "A Management By Objectives" and **Strategy Management**...

Every business is a system of processes that makes money, when:

- creates and delivers something of value,
- that other people want or need,
- at a price they are willing to pay,
- in a way that meets their needs and expectations,
- so that the business makes a profit for the benefit of partners, employees and operations.

But, before modeling this system of processes, we need to reflect on how the organization will achieve its purpose of existence and to reach the next stage of its evolution: the company's Mission and Vision.

Mission and Vision...just like I started this book. Such statements really matter, they must be well known by everyone and must always be visible.

Because, from this correct starting point, you will be presented with the first perspectives on customers, finances, internal processes and the company's learning and growth.

- What do we intend to do to reach more customers?
- To be financially successful?
- To satisfy the business processes in which we must achieve excellence?
- To sustain our ability to change and improve?

If any strategy is always going from point A to point B, considering different associated points of view, it will be enough to line up the strategic business objectives, followed by implementation of the tactical objectives, which will be executed through operational objectives, forming an adequate body of knowledge in the organization, with respective performances monitored in the long, medium and short terms. This way, we will achieve superior innovation and prompt problem solving.

That's how we've learned so far, right?!

Is that right? **No!**

Again...

Is that right? **No**, it doesn't work anymore!

In practice, it has proven to be an old statement: too theoretical, too formatted.

Maybe we are too used to just repeating this traditional model, from decades and decades in the past.

The quality we believe in must go far beyond directing, monitoring and critically analyzing internal and external issues; published annually in an extensive strategic planning document... as determined by well-known management manuals.

The wheel of the world turned and, for me, it worked according to the experience described below...

Each year, our strategic planning publication fell further behind in time, it was read less by employees and it had several excerpts repeated from previous versions, of the same unachieved objectives. Changing the text of the introduction or the organization of the index did not provide additional motivation for reading; neither did it reduce the number of pages.

The limit for accepting that something very wrong was progressing without question occurred when, almost at the end of the first half of a given year, the Board of Members had not yet approved the so-called "mandatory" (hierarchical) strategic planning document.

But the company continued to work very well on its objectives, reviewing its expected results, establishing new goals, positioning them over time and providing visibility at an appropriate frequency: they were real cycles of value creation, value delivery and of value capture.

So we arrive at Management By Objectives; and we consider A Management By Objectives to be truly strategic, when it itself has become our complete description of the business!

A challenging stance!

And a lot of things needed to be rethought and redone:

- from the Mission and Vision statements;
- supporting such Mission and Vision statements in actions;

- considering each discipline, skill and specialization contained in the Mission and Vision;
- guiding new executive guidelines for organizational policies;
- filling out the Business Model based on the expected objectives;
- relating objectives to values, customers, relationships, communications, activities, resources, partnerships, costs and revenues;
- clarifying, perfectly, "how we make money around here";
- eliminating, once and for all, the need for a traditional annual Strategic Planning;
- adapting a new reality of regular bi-monthly strategic planning;
- embracing new scenarios, internal and external, with each update;
- incorporating contributions from other management areas in each objective;
- fluidly evolving connected long, medium and short-term objectives;
- valuing specific, measurable, achievable, realistic and timely objectives(S.M.A.R.T.[1]);
- keeping the monitoring of other "KPIs", in addition to measuring and analyzing objectives and main results;
- aligning individuals' personal goals with the company's strategic initiatives;
- and, finally, inviting everyone to collaboration and professional recognition.

I therefore share this understanding: that the most natural objective of management by objectives is for it to be the complete strategy, for it to be the entire business.

How to manage a company? All answers above!

---
[1] https://en.wikipedia.org/wiki/Self-Monitoring,_Analysis_and_Reporting_Technology

Open a smile too! ;-)

Please note: it is no wonder that many "startups"[2] have been adopting OKRs as the key to their management model: make me think, don't tell me what to do; they use OKRs as a proposal for reflection, for analyzing problems and not as a repetition of the same formatted "cake recipe".

* * *

From "A Management By Objectives" and **Management By Processes**...

The best of both worlds: strategy and execution.

The fit I think is perfect.

Finally, a didactic (although simplified) definition for Integrated Management.

Integrated Management = Management By Processes + Management By Objectives

Above is the equation from my executive days! ;-)

Everything "horizontal", crossing the entire organization: processes and strategy... because modern corporate environments are no longer "vertical".

With Process Management, we solve:

- mapping business activities;
- those responsible for carrying out the activities;
- deliveries and pace of work products;
- management of communication between interested parties;
- quality assurance and control;

---

[2]https://en.wikipedia.org/wiki/Startup_company

- mitigating operational risks;
- escalation of issues and better relationships and
- automated solution for mature business processes.

However, in this interaction between processes, one must consider the existence of processes of very different granularities...

There are processes that see the business from afar, in an integral, holistic view; while other processes follow much more closely, focused on their specific, dedicated applications.

Bringing these different "sizes" of processes together into a single management culture solution does not bring us perfect cohesion, it does not keep the entire company indivisible, as desired. Unfortunately, there remains some unfilled space, a *"gap"*.

The glue, which guarantees such union, is, then, Management By Objectives.

And the gap, which will be filled, is Leadership Training.

With Management By Objectives "orbiting" the universe of Management By Processes, it becomes much more natural to resolve:

- strategic, tactical and operational objectives;
- corporate governance and financial controllership;
- the training plan and capabilities of work teams and
- decision management and business innovation.

Thus, with Process Management implemented, the assistant will continue carrying out his tasks, in compliance (and may be called, for example, "Process Responsible"); the analyst will evolve by preventing risks and errors, with greater critical sense (and may be named "Process Owner"); the manager will keep his attention focused on the harmony and performance of the group (being renamed "Owner of the Service")...but, only with the addition of a Management By Objectives, will everyone understand the pointing of the path, direction and the strategy, of a correct direction (or a new "Product Owner").

Now, imagine "Process Responsible", "Process Owner", "Service Owner" and "Product Owner", all together, defining and monitoring their respective objectives and main results!

Wow! In short, integrated management, training true "*champions*"!

Experience the approach to an end-to-end, data-driven operational excellence.

* * *

From "A Management By Objectives" and **Risk Management**...

A goal management system, accompanied by performance measurement. Objectives, targets, strategies and measures: these are our keywords. And don't forget: everything "S.M.A.R.T."[3], with specific, measurable, achievable, realistic and timely criteria.

A perfect model? What could go wrong? What are the unnoticed limitations?

Yes, there are chances of "side effects", of what "should never be done".

Note the risks below...

- "Unethical behavior": excessive concern with goals can, guaranteed, lead to more competition than collaboration, the retention of unshared information or ideas and changes in correct moral reasoning (through attitudes of fraud, dishonesty, purposeful reduction of quality, manipulation of numbers and statistics); with the sole intention of achieving the defined objective.

---

[3] https://en.wikipedia.org/wiki/Self-Monitoring,_Analysis_and_Reporting_Technology

- "No time for opportunities": the rush to prove numerical results allows new learning to go unnoticed, unexplored or without complete understanding; Routine, but essential, tasks can worsen performance, to the detriment of so-called special actions, more directly related to goals.
- "A simplified motivation": a broad work environment that thrives is not just about goals; It is impossible to establish an indicator that precisely quantifies the team's well-being, for example... even more so when there are goals with which an employee may not fully identify. If we achieve the goal, we are happy; if we don't achieve it, we become sad; life can't be just that...

In perfect illustration of these points, I admire the courage of the article "*I've never had a goal*"[4]), published in 2016, on the blog of the company Basecamp[5].

From the idea that summarizes the text, says the CEO Jason Fried[6]: "The reason most of us are unhappy, most of the time, is because we set our goals not for the person we will be when we achieve them, but we define our goals for the person we are when we set them."... a wonderful reflection! ;-)

A timely critique of "artificial goals", external and internal motivation and a welcome provocation of the time and space in which continuous improvement takes place!

Happiness is in the process towards the result, not the result itself.

Where do we want to get to? What's working? What's going wrong? What will we do differently? What are we learning?

These are the critical questions! So we need to talk more about people, please...bring me the next section soon!

* * *

---

[4] https://basecamp.com/articles/ive-never-had-a-goal
[5] https://brasil.basecamp.com/
[6] https://www.linkedin.com/in/jason-fried

From "A Management By Objectives" and **Management with People**...

It's easy to see examples of when achieving goals becomes toxic, an obsession.

Reflect, for a brief moment, and you will also remember something or someone...

I recently made an online purchase, with the deadline promised to be the same day...they just forgot to tell me that, until 23:59:59, it's still today (laughs)! And I imagine that no one appreciates being disturbed close to their bedtime. The obvious improvement solution would be to allow the user to set a specific time slot for site deliveries; but such a system of goals to be achieved has been ignoring reality for a long time, marketing is in full swing, holidays or Sundays are common days and no one has control over this accelerated chain in operation anymore... there is no way to stop it, you know?! Just stop buying at the store; who knew, they ran over the customer!

So I turn, once again, to Jason Fried, because I also like the title of his 2020 book: "It Doesn't Have to Be Crazy at Work"[7].

In this scenario, of necessary debate about clarity, purpose, sustainable rhythm and balance, the "OKRs" architecture brings us a complementary solution, of great value to the model: the "CFRs": "*Conversation*", "* Feedback*", "*Recognition*".

"CFRs" therefore resolve the gap already presented ("if we reach the objective, we are happy; if we don't reach it, we are sad") and guarantee a healthy evolution of OKRs, considering people: their behaviors and their results!

In fact, the full title of this system should be: "OKRs and CFRs" (not just "OKRs"), as the fundamental importance of CFRs must be valued more, in support of the proposed model.

---

[7] https://www.amazon.com/Doesnt-Have-Be-Crazy-Work/dp/B07G8L5NZ9

The proposal is that such meetings take place in a "1 to 1" format, in a private conversation between a higher authority and its subordinate, based on a critical analysis of the delivery of the intended objectives, a review of the processes used and a retrospective of partial results.

It is the desired solution for training leaders and gaining maturity throughout the organization, in continuous management of personal performance; a transition from the decadent model of rewards and bonuses to a transparent meritocracy and appreciation of competencies (knowledge, skills and attitudes).

I'll explain more below, in "PART V", "Integrated Coordination"...

For now, John Doerr's quote remains: "Ideas are easy; execution is everything."

* * *

From "A Management By Objectives" and **Commercial and Financial Management**...

Although the world needs more companies focused on quality, we cannot stop focusing on profit.

We all follow a usual income cycle, with revenue planning, execution of the financial routine and financial monitoring, for the desired profit; respecting the differences of each industry in which it operates.

And, to make sure that the money is under control, there are several possibilities for measurement indicators.

In some examples, below.

- Conquer a new consumer market.
- Transform our sales team into the best in the industry.

- Make our company always more profitable.
- Develop remote work to reduce office expenses.

Marketing, sales and financial information: we also seek, through Management By Objectives, to monitor a broad financial relationship with customers.

And, based on these simplified examples, it is clear that OKRs are, in themselves, an excellent Financial Controlling tool, monitoring corporate governance and demonstrating Decision Management.

PART II THE HEART OF THE STRATEGY

Why?

"To dream the impossible dream, to fight the unbeatable foe, to bear with unbearable sorrow, to run where the brave dare not go, to right the unrightable wrong, to be better afar than you are, to try when your arms are too weary, to reach the unreachable star: this is my quest!" – Elvis Presley, "The Impossible Dream"

The easy question: what do you want to have?

The hard question: what do you **want to be**?

Because "having" will always come up against concrete limits.

Think about your examples, without guilt…

And **because** "being" is infinite, continuous!

A more difficult reflection, right?!

Now applying it to business…

Because strategy is not "how?" and it will never be "what?".

This is a very basic, very common and very amateur mistake!

Believing in the strategy, thinking about "how?" or "what?," is a simplified, superficial and therefore imprecise and inefficient view.

Yes, the strategy will always be the **"why"**!

Because the strategy needs to come from the heart!

It's a dream to come true, you know?

From the dictionary, "inspire": provoke ideas, thoughts; give birth to creative enthusiasm.

Now, our "body" is more awake to move forward, with our heart beating faster!

Commitment to Mission and Vision

"Hello again, it's you and me. Kinda always like it used to be. Sippin' wine, killing time. Trying to solve life's mysteries. How's your life, it's been a while?! God, it's good to see you smile. If you go now, I'll understand. If you stay, hey, I've gotta plan. You wanna make a memory? You can sing the melody to me. And I can write a couple lines. You wanna make a memory?" – Bon Jovi, "Make A Memory"

We've asked the difficult question (what do you want to be?), but we haven't answered it yet...

Don't worry, it's not that difficult and it's more practical and objective than you think, too.

Observe the excerpts highlighted in retrospective of my **Vision**, already presented in the introduction of this book...

"I seek to establish a career as a **author of business books**, accompanied by the offering of training, lectures, consultancy and mentoring; through extensive content of my own, recognized innovative performance, continuous creative solutions and a real delivery of value to those who work with me. reserve their time and attention. The proposal is that we all follow an **executive path of leadership**, reputation and better business results in renewed partnership and trust. One day, I intend to be **your favorite author**."

From the well-known hobby "find the words in the text", we then find: "author of business books", "executive leadership trajectory" and "your favorite author"; which can thus be transformed into agile writing of objectives, listed below.

Commitment to Mission and Vision

- Consolidating an international career as an author of business books.
- Be a national reference for the topic of executive leadership.
- Living off the income from my writing in financial independence.

Vision and Objectives directly related, right?!

A grateful and strong cohesion!

Which can still be validated by the complementary analysis of the **Mission**.

"I write about everything that I wish someone had already written and that I also missed reading. I only communicate about what I have already lived, experienced, learned, made mistakes and needed to organize in my head, for a *better professional performance *. I write and communicate with theory and practice, balancing the simple and the complex, for a **better business world** May my books also **promote your career**, your job, your team, your work sector. and your company."

Do you want to practice another exercise like this?

Below is the Vision of the company I work as CEO...

"May our **medical excellence** and our **management excellence** be perceived **by you**. May offering the **most accurate** and **fastest** anatomopathological diagnosis make a difference **in society**. May leadership, reputation and innovation be **validated by quality**".

Translating into Objectives, we will have:

- Be recognized for the medical excellence of the most accurate anatomopathological report;
- Be recognized for excellence in managing the fastest anatomopathological report;
- Be profitable through proven quality as a strategic differentiator.

Proving, once again, the exercise as a complement to the Mission:

"We work for answers, for truth, for everything that is real. We always work harder, better and for all of us. We work in science in the service of health and with respect for life."

As we wanted to demonstrate!

And it's usually like this: 3 big goals are enough for us…you just need to know "where to look" and align "with your heart".

Please do not waste any time on the internet researching and copying other people's goals, goals stated in free .PDF files, or goals from popular MBA classrooms; do learn how to write good and personalized Mission and Vision statements, which favor the strategic development of your business Objectives!

Exactly "in practice", as proposed: our purpose for existing, strengthens what we want to be; Mission and Vision remain indivisible, atomic and guiding the Objectives!

The "difficult" question is partially answered. Key Results (Part III) and Initiatives (Part IV) will complement our approach to A Management By Objectives.

More Objective Examples

"Breathe, breathe in the air. Don't be afraid to care. Leave, but don't leave me. Look around. And choose your own ground. For long you live and high you fly. And smiles you'll give and tears you'll cry. And all you touch and all you see. Is all your life will ever be." – Pink Floyd, "Breathe (In The Air)"

Ok, we already understand that goals must be **ambitious** and that they can, indeed, seem a little uncomfortable, at first.

But be sure to set ambitious and uncomfortable goals: reaching **70%** of completion, for a goal, is already a good result!

Note that objectives should not contain any number or metric in their description: it would be a serious error, confusing guidance, an insecure conceptualization.

Objectives must be **qualitative**! Never quantitative…

If desired, objectives can indeed include a determined **deadline** that drives action. Annual, quarterly objectives…

Also, don't exceed a maximum of **5** objectives! After all, there must be sufficient management over them. The well known term *"the vital few"*.

These are just the basic rules, the premises of strong requirements, but without going too far into rigidity or purism.

Freely, there can be objectives for countless actions: for your team, your work sector or your company.

Sales, Finance, Marketing, HR, Purchasing, Logistics, Research and Development, Engineering, Legal…

They can be suggested from higher hierarchies to lower levels and vice versa!

More Objective Examples

And objectives can serve to shield: opportunities and strengths to explore, weaknesses and threats to mitigate, financial, customer, process or learning perspectives.

So, here are some more examples, as a welcome inspiration.

- Reach historic record for increased profitability.
- Surpass last quarter's sales.
- Consolidate participation throughout the national market.
- Innovate by opening new profitable business fronts.
- Attract and retain the best talents to work in the company.
- Continuously improve statistical control operations.
- To be the leading brand in our industry.

From customers, performance, revenue, growth, engagement: improvise!

PART III THE BRAIN OF TACTICS

How?

"We repeat that we want it, but we don't look for it, and, in an abstract way, we delude ourselves that we truly did it."–Oswaldo Montenegro, "Quebra-Cabeça Sem Luz"

Let's think a little more to achieve a goal...

And let's talk about numbers!

From the acronym OKR, "Objective" correctly and appropriately represents "Why?" and "Key Result" is the "How?".

Hence, we arrive at a very commonly used wording, in this management by objectives:

"My goal is [...], measured through [...]".

Key Results must always be measurable and must be easy to evaluate with a number!

Numbers, because Key Results, unlike Objectives, are quantitative.

Key Results are goals with metrics.

To avoid doubt: metrics are measures of performance; and measurements, in turn, are quantities in their units of magnitude.

Thus, **metrics are specific measurements**, extrapolated to monitor the achievement of objectives.

In very basic examples: "climb 3 mountains", "eat 5 pies" etc.

But remember to ideally determine three Key Results per Objective.

Therefore, in a more extended version of the standard OKRs writing, we will have:

"My goal is [...], during the period of [...], measured through [...], [...] and [...]".

How?

A good capacity suggestion is to have three to five objectives per quarter, carrying three to five key results each.

Or accept the risk of teams being overworked or misaligned in their efforts...

And, to correctly calculate the progress of each Key Result, we will then need to define three values: the initial value, the goal value and the current value.

Because the initial value is not always zero!

Progress = (([Current Value] - [Initial Value]) / ([Goal Value] - [Initial Value])) * 100

In any exercises, below.

- Reduce losses to 14%.
- Target Value: 14%.
- Initial Value: 20%.
- Current Value: 16%.
- Progress = ((16 - 20) / (14 - 20)) * 100
- Progress = 67%

Another exercise...

- Increase earnings to 20%.
- Target Value: 20%.
- Initial Value: 14%.
- Current Value: 16%.
- Progress = ((16 - 14) / (20 - 14)) * 100
- Progress = 33%

Just some basic math, so there are no doubts!

Project Planning

"Ridin' down the highway. Goin' to a show. Stop in all the byways. Playin' rock 'n' roll. Gettin' robbed. Gettin' stoned. Gettin' beat up. Broken-boned. Gettin' had. Gettin' took. I tell you, folks. It's harder than it looks. It's a long way to the top if you wanna rock 'n' roll. It's a long way to the top if you wanna rock 'n' roll. ... If you think it's easy doin' one night stands. Try playin' in a rock roll band. It's a long way to the top if you wanna rock 'n' roll." – AC/DC, "It's A Long Way To The Top"

From the clarified concepts, consider that we already have a project in hand!

A project is any initiative, to be carried out in adherence to a desired development and management process, for the successful delivery of a product or service.

We now need to implement our **objective management system project, monitoring the performance of main strategic results.**

A beautiful document title, isn't it?! ;-)

The most important thing is that our project reflects your entrepreneurial nature and brings a lot of innovation; This way, it will be even more beautiful!

Below, I present the sequence of activities that will make up the development process suggested for this type of project:

- Establish and maintain commitment,
- Plan the measurement,
- Perform the measurement,
- Evaluate the measurement and its communication.

Project Planning

Each of these steps will be detailed throughout this book; and correspond, in direct association, to common phases of the project management discipline:

- Initiation,
- Planning,
- Development and
- Control and Monitoring.

In this didactic, well-organized way, it will be easier to understand its progress and all its details.

It's a life cycle proposal: with a beginning, a middle, but no end!

* * *

"Don't Push the River: It Flows by Itself": I love the title of this book, by the psychologist Barry Stevens[1]!

It's like arriving at the airport very early: everyone expects a smooth takeoff.

At this moment, in our project, we are at the beginning, in the initiation phase.

And if it were a game...

Does everyone know the rules?

Will everyone respect the rules?

Is everyone excited to play?

Let's play together?

Shall we play differently?

Shall we celebrate together?

But how did I do it, in my company?! In practice, I will list the initial steps below...

---

[1] https://en.wikipedia.org/wiki/Barry_Stevens_(therapist)

- Schedule a short meeting: 1 hour is enough;
- Invite as many people as possible: make the event important, multidisciplinary and democratic;
- Dedicate half of the meeting to briefly explain the highlights already mentioned so far in this book;
- Talk a little about everything: management by objectives, strategy management, process management, risk management, people management, commercial and financial management;
- With everyone already comfortable (and aligned) in the session, move on to the second half of the meeting: the new management model, 100% goal-oriented;
- Talk about well-known companies that already adopt this approach;
- Value the possibility of balancing objectives: individual and corporate;
- Highlight how leadership processes (strategy, decision, capacity, innovation, technology, investment, viability, accounting, etc.) tend to be restricted to senior management and company management, being barely visible;
- In comparison, highlight how much other processes (administration, regularity, communication, maintenance, people, accounts payable, accounts receivable, relationships, quality control, etc.) obtain habitual and greater operational participation;
- Demonstrate how an isolated indicator measurement is very different from an indicator measurement driven by objectives and the strength of the set (perhaps the clearest difference between just working on "KPIs" and maturing them through "OKRs");
- Then, open the meeting for a broad debate of different examples: on how everything could be reviewed from a new perspective and compass of objectives and collaboration;

Project Planning

- Events, incidents, problems, obstacles, interests: a huge "brainstorming" about where we want to go and how we want to get there;
- End the meeting as your greatest experience of collective strategic planning in real time;
- There is no need here for any planning yet: just ensure that, in the end, everyone leaves feeling special and invited to the new project;
- Now, we are part of something great; and we will never accept anything less!

So please read these topics, again…with a smile! ;-)

Each item listed is very important and sets the stage for successful implementation to come.

* * *

Plans on paper (after all the information collected in the previous experience).

Understand: every plan is about the actions of a model.

The model is just a representation or a simplified interpretation of reality; while the plan evaluates and builds the path from where we are to where we want to go.

Models are static and plans are dynamic: the plan is the rational side of the model!

Hahaha, I love these conceptual reviews; which also bring clarity to my reasoning, naming things correctly.

The funniest thing is that, in previous studies on OKRs, I found little detailed planning for their implementation…

Most of the references always seemed limited to me: some added usage statements or even unnecessary complexity.

The current moment therefore requires some dose of courage, in presenting a true and reusable case report.

Let's formalize "why" and "how" the work will be, based on an experienced example.

Provide all participants with an adequate understanding of the process, in adherence.

Present information clearly and consistently.

In the following 3 sections, we have: "established objectives", "main results defined prioritized and documented" and "specified collection and analysis procedures"...that's our planning!

* * *

Established objectives...

In the most formal way: **tactical measurement objectives are defined based on strategic objectives and information needs, to advance the business processes.**

What is at stake, at this moment, is that there must be some document registration and that this document obtains both the collaboration of those involved and the approval of the company's senior management: a broad and reliable sponsorship.

Collaboration is something new here, right?!

And, as stated, the objectives must continue to be regularly reviewed and adapted; Therefore, the deadline that will differentiate a strategic objective from a tactical objective will always be a configuration of the organization, without any rigor in understanding what short, medium and long terms represent.

Strategic objectives, as already seen, are not difficult to record, as they demonstrate many similarities, even for different industries or different sizes of organization.

The beauty of the new model is, then, in the tactical objectives: they are the focus and the key to planning success!

Creativity remains free, in the well-known standard statement: "My objective is [...], measured through [...]", always favoring a clear binary answer and always accompanied by the evidence of numbers.

Ready! This is the expected outcome of your executive document's presentation panel: an established agreement on the Objectives ("O") and their Key Results ("KR").

It sounds simple, but it cannot be simplified; It must be simple so that we can know it by heart, to keep it active in our memory: it is for every day and for every task!

Oh, in the next external quality audit (accreditation), how I would like to be asked about which "OKR" I am working on and contributing to, instead of answering whether I know the annual strategic objectives... it is a fact that the world has turned!

It is also a fact that there are already many applications and software developed to make this ecosystem of goals and metrics easier: as you progress through the tutorial you will ensure adherence to the conceptual model... but still within the pre-established limits and boundaries of the tool.

Although a solution based on spreadsheets and reports exported to PDF seems very manual and slower, it does strengthen learning and new information architectures: initially, we just don't want to automate any errors.

This stage ends with the well-known "captain's voice": in communication, by the leadership, of the established objectives.

*   *   *

Main Results defined, prioritized and documented...

Starting, again, with the formalization of the expected practice of our process: **an appropriate set of measures, guided by the established objectives, is defined, prioritized and documented.**

Yes, for each objective, we will have one or more main results!

Obviously, at least one; however, it is unlikely that we will have only one main result in direct correlation with an objective.

It is natural that, to complete a challenging and agile objective, it is necessary to complement several results (otherwise, perhaps, your objective would be smaller)... so, let's combine the main ones!

Main Results defined, prioritized and documented have the force of a contract for the objective: they are activities that need to be conducted, in synergy, so that the common goal can be declared as completed, as ready.

"One for all and all for one".

Such selection itself requires prioritization and communications... exactly like a contract.

Therefore, from this perception of the contract, the most extended version of the standard statement for OKRs emerges, seeking to make everything even clearer in its evolution:

"My goal is [...], during the period of [...], measured through [...], [...] and [...]".

The strength of "A Management By Objectives" added to "Management with People" is now decisive, in necessary interdisciplinary action.

From there, everything gets easier: to identify Key Results, start by relating different leaders to the Objectives!

Leadership and Key Results will also favor the balance between individual and corporate interests: collaboration is very welcome here!

Project Planning

As anticipated, we manage for happiness!

* * *

Procedures for collection and analysis specified...

How to collect the data? Automatically (preferential) or manually? At what collection frequency? From which data sample? Is it a reliable, representative sample? Is the data a continuous value, based on a numerical count or a categorized classification?

How to analyze the data? What type of graphics to represent it? A histogram, trend or bar chart? With some descriptive statistics, in addition to graphical analysis? What components will form our statistical control? Setpoint, minimum, maximum and average? Standard deviation?

What is the origin of this data? What are your units of measurement? How can two people inform the same data, without relevant variations? And how will they be able to interpret the analyzes in a similar way?

There are 17 important questions to answer!

Like this...

Procedures for the collection, storage and analysis of key results need to be specified; to train those responsible for execution and to form a safe and correct historical database... because, here, nothing can be subjective!

Google uses a straightforward scoring scale, from 0.0 to 1.0, which is purely mathematical.

From the completion percentages of their associated key results, the arithmetic average of these percentage rates is calculated to score the objective.

In example:

Progress % KR = (Progress % KR1 + Progress % KR2 + Progress % KR3) / 3

This explains the need for every key result to carry its own number, in target and in monitoring: hence, no interpretations in the partial calculation of the percentage of completion.

If from 0.7 to 1.0, the situation is green ("we delivered").

If from 0.4 to 0.6, the situation is yellow ("we've made progress, but it's not ready").

If from 0.0 to 0.3, the situation is red ("we have not achieved significant progress").

Very interesting, because:

- is easy to manage visually: green, yellow and red;
- does not invalidate the debate, process review or lessons learned;
- establishes consensus on an objective conclusion, from which more subjective interpretations begin;
- in addition to subtly incorporating conceptual rigor into the writing of OKRs (we need numbers).

And, at the end of this planning stage, we will then have moved towards preparing our own "scoreboard": with a model ready for filling out and execution, feeding a rich, personalized executive summary of the business.

The central idea: we are not machines; teach us the process (do not impose the process on us), follow and adapt the process (then we will learn together).

The Key Results

"If I want to talk to God, I have to venture out. I have to climb to the heavens, without ropes to hold on. I have to say goodbye, turn my back, walk; decided, for the road, which, when it ends, will lead to nothing. Nothing, nothing, nothing, nothing; nothing, nothing, nothing, nothing; nothing, nothing, nothing, nothing that I thought I would find." –Gilberto Gil,("Se Eu Quiser Falar Com Deus").

How do we know if we have achieved our objective?

This is the definitive question, which we are working on so much in this chapter.

And, as we begin to execute the procedures for collection and analysis, detailed in the previous chapter, we will notice a subtle but fundamental difference in the nature of some Key Results: whether they allow us only a **"retroactive control"** or a **"projected warranty"**.

From "retroactive control", we understand that the new measurement will only provide feedback to the system, which, based on this obtained value, will continue seeking the goal through the new reality: there is always a *"lag"* intrinsic to this type of Key Result, as it is only known after the end of the determined period of time.

From the "projected guarantee", we realize that we are continually evaluating the expected future condition of the Key Result: there is a *"lead"* acting, in real time on this type of Key Result, which can be corrected during the established period of time.

Thus, Key Results *"lag"* or *"lead"* are **both** useful.

Every set of Key Results, which supports a given Objective, must present a pleasant **balance** between *"lag"* and *"lead"* Key Results.

The Key Results

An important concept and an important strategy for success in your Management By Objectives!

Otherwise, imagine if everything was only discovered at the end of the quarter? It would almost be a "Baby Shower"[1] for OKRs (laughs): not always the creative way of revealing the baby's gender to parents, friends and family happen according to each person's expectations.

* * *

To end the chapter, here are some real examples of Key Results...

Many defend writing Key Results starting with verbs, such as: increase, decrease, reduce, achieve, move, launch, activate, maintain, etc.

It's a nice idea, which I like and have already used: there's nothing wrong with it.

But, over time, I ended up being, naturally, attracted to the intuitive use of **relational mathematical operators**, in my much more direct and necessarily numerical statements.

- "<" less than
- ">" greater than
- "=" equal to
- "!=" not equal to
- "<=" less than or equal to
- ">=" greater than or equal to

A personal "essentialist" approach[2] for my KRs!

I think it's worth trying, too!

---

[1] https://en.wikipedia.org/wiki/Baby_shower
[2] https://en.wikipedia.org/wiki/Essentialism

The Key Results

So, I came up with some personal examples, which I genuinely share below.

Objective 1...

- Objective: To consolidate an international career as an author of business books.
- Key Result: Published translations = 5.
- Key Result: Language study sessions = 150.

Objective 2...

- Objective: To be a national reference for the topic of executive leadership.
- Key Result: Readings completed in leadership = 5.
- Key Result: Hours in internal mentoring sessions = 100.

Objective 3...

- Objective: To live off the income from my writing in financial independence.
- Key Result: Pages written = 300.
- Key Result: Amazon Royalties = 10,000.
- Key Result: Amazon KENP = 60,000

And, just like Objectives, it is very easy to derive results for any area of activity in your company: sales, finance, marketing, HR, purchasing, logistics, R&D, engineering, legal, etc.

In summary...

Achieving a Goal must always be a binary answer: zero or one, true or false, yes or no.

Tracking a Key Result must be an analogue trajectory: made up of numbers in natural variation.

The indicator will show us this path!

PART IV THE BODY IN ACTION

O quê?

"Every day she takes a morning bath, she wets her hair. Wraps a towel around her as she's heading for the bedroom chair. It's just another day. Slipping into stockings, stepping into shoes. Dipping in the pocket of her raincoat. It's just another day. At the office, where the papers grow, she takes a break. Drinks another coffee and she finds it hard to stay awake. It's just another day." – Paul McCartney, "Another Day"

Ideally, it would be to solve your life in a single day, right? Everything adjusted, in full order, from today to tomorrow! ;-)

It's also easy to work, with dedication, for 1 month or 1 year: very few employees ruin everything the day after the job interview, right?

However, maintaining excellence and rhythm, daily, for 10, 20, 30 years, is a much more challenging task!

It is therefore worth noting: staying at the top requires a lot of effort and adaptation and is a condition of adult life, for the longevity of individuals and legal entities.

We now need to **value actions** of creating, maintaining or repairing something.

When John Doerr says that "ideas are easy, execution is everything", I understand it in an "extended" way: success, indeed, will not be limited to the project implementation milestone ("Part III"); because there will still be a long way to go to sustain this implementation.

Or, from the new phrase I learned, "the fastest way, between the idea and the results, is called execution" (Camila Farani).

And here we are: get to work!

Business Process Management

"I don't know what I've been livin' on, but. It's not enough to fill me up. I need more than just words can say. I need everything this life can give me. 'Cause something reached out and touched me. Now I know all I want. I want the best of both worlds." –Van Halen, "Best Of Both Worlds"

The integrated management of a great place to work...

Integrated Management = Management By Processes + Management By Objectives.

In a presentation of our Management By Objectives, associated with Management By Processes, we defined Integrated Management as a result, in a chapter in Part I of this book.

It is therefore desired that all work is based on processes, that every employee is trained in the process in which they work and that there is proven academic training for the respective area of knowledge.

Areas of knowledge are identified from the Mission and Vision statements and guarantee the writing of their Organizational Policies.

Processes are planned from Organizational Policies, deriving a first general process, a macro process that summarizes the entire production of goods or services, the Value Chain.

From there, follow:

- provision of resources,
- allocation of responsibilities,

- activity training,
- control of work products,
- involvement of all interested parties,
- monitoring processes,
- adherence to objectives and
- review of key results.

Such a grand project is called Organizational Culture!

It is the biggest, only objective of all results-based management.

And its atomic, indivisible element, which will guarantee all the desired cohesion force, is represented by people!

I would therefore like to take this opportunity to list some selected questions, for timely and complementary reflection, below.

- Do people realize their importance in contributing to results?
- Are people encouraged to balance corporate and individual goals?
- Do people dedicate the time agreed with the company to routine work and key results?
- Do people communicate their ideas and suggestions for better results?
- Can people ask any reasonable question and get straight answers?
- Do people understand unintentional mistakes as part of learning for results?
- Do people have a clear vision of where they are going and how they will get there?
- Do people feel like they are all "in the same boat"?
- Are people willing to give more of themselves to advance a key result?
- Are people willing to collaborate to complete a goal?
- Are people honest and ethical in driving their key results?
- Do people avoid "politicking" as a way of advancing results?

- Do people work emotionally healthy, contributing to objectives?
- Are people kept informed of the main results and changes in objectives?
- Are people recognized for good work and extra effort?
- Does everyone have the opportunity to receive special recognition?
- Do people celebrate completed goals?
- Is recognition given to people who truly deserve it most?

It is because of the behavioral and interpersonal skills ("*soft skills*"), added to the technical skills ("*hard skills*"), that you will never agree to participate in anything smaller again!

The Initiatives

"Hold life I'm gonna live it up. I'm taking flight, I said I'll never get enough. Stand tall, I'm young and kinda proud. I'm on the top as long as the music's loud. If you think I'll sit around as the world goes by. You're thinking like a fool, cause it's a case of do or die. Out there is a fortune waiting to be had. If you think I'll let it go, you're mad. You've got another thing coming. You've got another thing coming!" – Judas Priest, "You've Got Another Thing Coming"

"Initiatives" correspond to the work needed to be done to achieve the OKR ("yes" and "no" or % completion).

So, **how to connect BPM and OKRs**?

After all, that is the subtitle of the book!

How to connect Management By Processes and Management By Objectives?

In practice, it works like this…

- Identify process areas: processes exist and are everywhere; you must know how to bring them together.
- Expand your hierarchy horizontally: for each process, a Process Leader; for each process area, a Service Leader (responsible for process leaders); for the entire package, a Product Leader (responsible for service leaders)…it is a lean functional structure and no one will work disconnected from the processes.
- For each process, work may arise, daily, as a recurring process activity ceremony, a problem, an incident, an event, an improvement, a performance impediment; but also as a **key results initiative**… the strategy is guaranteed to be incorporated into operations.

- Yes, spread the OKRs initiatives into the established knowledge of process management, to take care of this explosion of granularity: 3 objectives * 3 key results/objective * 12 initiatives/key result = 108 initiatives per quarter.

As a result...

- Every day, we meet, briefly, and establish the **contract** of the "Day's Action Plans", for the team's **processes**, based on the selection of the **task list** (as stated: a recurring ceremony of process activity, a problem, an incident, an event, an improvement, a performance impediment, a key result initiative);
- Every month, we also meet, with a little more time, and review the performance indicators of the entire organization (feeding more action plans to the task list).

In short, a **managed environment**: at pace, commitment, adaptation and constantly evolving key results.

This is my **continuous improvement of OKRs and BPM**: and it works great!

Examples of Initiatives

"Give me your hand, I'd like to shake it. I want to show you I'm your friend. You'll understand. If I can make it clear. It's all that matters in the end. Put it there if it weighs a ton. That's what a father said to his young son. I don't care if it weighs a ton. As long as you and I are here, put it there. Long as you and I are here, put it there."–Paul McCartney, "Put It There"

Do it! Just like the introductory text of this book!

Value initiatives! Because, without them, nothing, nothing happens!

Initiatives are the driving force of the entire model, but, interestingly, initiatives correspond to the least detailed component in almost all OKR texts!

Simply because most still don't understand how to connect them, in practice, to routine objectives and key results.

For a long time, I also had this doubt, which I resolved through the strategic integration of OKRs into the Business Process Management ("BPM") operation.

I do not believe it is effective to measure and monitor the "top-down" structure (Objectives > Key Results > Initiatives).

I believe that the best performance and the guarantee of implementation success happen "from the bottom up" (Initiatives > Key Results > Objectives).

So, complementing some of my personal OKRs, shared in the previous chapter, I understand the need for more examples, please, below.

Objective 1...

Examples of Initiatives

- Objective: To consolidate an international career as an author of business books.
- Key Result: Published translations = 5.
- Initiative: Translate Book 3 ES.
- Initiative: Publish Book 3 ES Kindle, Print and Hardcover.
- Initiative: Translate Book 3 EN.
- Initiative: Publish Book 3 EN Kindle, Print and Hardcover.
- Initiative: Update translation new edition Book 1 ES.
- Initiative: Republish Book 1 ES Kindle, Print and Hardcover.
- Initiative: Publish Book 2 ES Print Hardcover.
- Initiative: Publish Series 1 ES Management in Practice Kindle, Print and Hardcover.
- Initiative: Translate Book 2 EN.
- Initiative: Publish Book 2 EN Kindle, Print and Hardcover.
- Initiative: Publish Book 1 EN Print Hardcover.
- Initiative: Publish Series 1 EN Management in Practice Kindle, Print and Hardcover.

Objective 2...

- Objective: To live off the income from my writing in financial independence.
- Key Result: Amazon Royalties = 10,000.
- Initiative: Publish Book 3 PT Kindle, Print and Hardcover.
- Initiative: Republish Book 1 PT Kindle, Print and Hardcover.
- Initiative: Publish Book 2 PT Print Hardcover.
- Initiative: Publish Series 1 PT Management in Practice Kindle, Print and Hardcover.
- Initiative: Prepare TEACHABLE environment Book 1 PT.
- Initiative: Publish 6 working hour course Book 1 PT.
- Initiative: Prepare TEACHABLE environment Book 2 PT.
- Initiative: Publish 6 working hour course Book 3 PT.
- Initiative: Prepare TEACHABLE environment Book 3 PT.
- Initiative: Publish 6 working hour course Book 3 PT.

Examples of Initiatives

- Initiative: Publish own audiobook narration 1 PT.
- Initiative: Publish own audiobook narration 2 PT.
- Initiative: Publish own audiobook narration 3 PT.

"As We Wanted to Demonstrate", be careful with this real explosion of granularity (approximately 12 initiatives/key result per quarter) and I see no better strategy than incorporating key result initiatives into the company's routine. process management!

PART V INTEGRATED COORDINATION

When?

"When the road looks rough ahead. And you're miles and miles. From your nice warm bed. You just remember what your old pal said. Boy, you've got a friend in me. Yeah, you've got a friend in me." – Randy Newman, "You've Got a Friend In Me"

At the end of every project, we have a **service** result to maintain.

Projects and services are very different from each other: projects have a beginning, middle and end, while services are continuous; Projects are developed progressively, and services are repeated every day.

Let's then establish our service timeline, our **"rituals"** or ceremonies, based on the key elements in the process of designing and implementing OKRs.

Here, the values are in alignment, priority, monitoring and sustainability!

- Start of the quarter: **"Definition of OKRs"** – configuration and alignment of OKRs with the strategy and stakeholders.
- Continuously: **"Check Ins"** – to update the progress of OKRs, record partial results and support.
- On an ongoing basis: **"Coaching"** – for comments and recognition.
- Weekly/Fortnightly/Monthly: **"Cadence Reviews"** – formal conversations to share progress, impediments, updates, ensure pacing and gain commitment (reasons for progress, what's working, what's not working, what we are learning, what are the action plans).
- Quarterly: **"Retrospectives"** - planning for the next quarter (which OKRs will be transferred; what's new; lessons learned from the previous quarter; reflections and changes).

Define, align, record, review, reflect, reset. Define, align, record, review, reflect, reset. Define, align, record, review, reflect, reset.

An **iterative process** (cycles of repetition and accumulation of experiences), of necessary executive sponsorship, "*coaching*", "*feedback*", recognition, collaboration and discipline.

But, although this is the standard in the OKRs structure, with well-defined, fixed and synchronized time intervals per quarter, nothing prevents the team from opting for a more continuous flow; frequently asking yourself: "have we achieved it yet?", "have we achieved it yet?", "have we achieved it yet?". I confess that I like this **alternative approach!** ;-)

"CFRs": Conversations, Feedback, Recognition

"*Coaching*" is not mentoring ("that's how I would do it...").

"*Coaching*" is not counseling ("try doing it this way...").

"*Coaching*" is not psychotherapy ("why have you been acting like this?").

"*Coaching*" is not training ("learn to do it like this...").

"*Coaching*" is not consultancy ("that's how it should be done...").

"*Coaching*" is a process of change and transformation, focusing on future possibilities!

And "*coaching*" has a direct consequence on leadership development!

Indeed, for years I have been running **individual meetings**, one by one, director and collaborator, always conducted based on a prior personalized script of a mental map of ideas to be presented, with the balance of evolving the Management By Processes, the

When?

Management By Objectives and the professional development of the employee.

The objective is to invite collaborations to initiatives that improve organizational policies. Regardless of positions and hierarchies, the aim is to train leaders in different areas of business knowledge, distributed across work teams.

Below is my planned and current structure...

(10 min) Where do we want to get to? What's working? What's going wrong? What will we do differently? What are we learning?

(10 min) Constructive behavior + Results achieved? Advance! Defensive behavior + Results achieved? Redefine! Constructive behavior + Unachieved results? Redefine! Defensive behavior + Unachieved results? Line up!

(20 min) Behavior? Impact? Action plans!

(10 min) Behavior? Effect? Recognition!

Yes, you will also need to build your **coaching culture**!

"*Coaching*" = educate, plan, organize, think strategically, negotiate, facilitate, listen (facts, feelings, intentions, values, beliefs, qualities), communicate.

We all continue in grateful partnership!

One plus one is greater than two ($1 + 1 > 2$), understand?!

Measurement and Communication

"It's a machine's world. Don't tell me I ain't got no soul. When the machines take over. It ain't no place for rock 'n' roll..." - Queen, "Machines (Back To Humans)"

Measurement

Perhaps, for Google, it will be much easier than for us! (laughter)

After all, Google's own Mission has been to "organize the world's information so that it is universally accessible and useful"... regardless of whether they already used OKRs or not.

Like this,

- set a goal,
- align your key results
- and configure your collection, presentation and analysis It may seem automatic, immediate and trivial ... but it's not!

It would only be automatic, immediate and trivial if all the necessary data were always there, available, in the appropriate format, for any necessary integration.

And this is obviously not the common reality of most companies and it is no surprise that John Doerr's book does not detail the implementation of this chapter.

The required data must be **collected** and **analyzed**, as planned; and that requires effort!

Sometimes, this step requires additional analyses, reviewing the results with stakeholders, better refining the identification of the main results or better defining the relationship of the analyzes to the measurement objectives.

The data and analysis results also need to be **stored**, making it possible to construct and review your historical series.

Along with the data and results, contextual information must be presented, enough to guide its understanding and interpretation.

In the next sections, I will then present you with two execution solutions: one manual and freely customized; the other, more automatic and with pre-established parameters to be configured.

A particular choice, both with advantages and disadvantages, to be noted.

A small improvement project on A4 paper

Indeed, the tool I reuse the most fits on a single A4 sheet!

Okay, two pages actually: front and back. (laughter)

And everything that is lean makes me very happy! ;-)

It is the approach of a small improvement project, embedded in each performance indicator of organizational measurement, in desired conceptual adherence to the DMAIC model, from Six Sigma[1]: • Define, • Measure, • Analyze, • Improve and • Control.

Start from the electronic spreadsheet *"template"* defined by your company.

The "cover" must be simple: just list all OKRs worked, according to the standard statement already studied. Also include an "executive

---

[1] https://en.wikipedia.org/wiki/Six_Sigma

panel", with a summary of the visual results (green, yellow or red) of the indicators: target, current value and percentage of progress.

From then on, follow one indicator per page; like the step by step below.

Ensure an initial section, in the page header, with context information for the **DEFINITION** of the problem; in suggested fields:

- Goal;
- Main results;
- Perspective (customers, finances, internal processes or learning) and
- Employees ("Management By Objectives Committee").

Questions could also be listed about the costs arising from any associated low quality.

In the next section of the document, present the procedures on how to collect the **MEASUREMENT**:

- Automatic or Manual;
- Collection frequency;
- Quantity of samples;
- Data type ("continuous", "count" or "classification");
- Chart type ("histogram", "trend chart" or "bars").

From the **ANALYSIS** stage, consider:

- Minimum descriptive statistics ("average", "minimum historical value" and "maximum historical value");
- Objective score ("goal", "initial value", "current value" and "percentage of progress");
- Data plotted on a graph;
- Answers to "Five Whys[2]", down to the root cause.

---

[2] https://en.wikipedia.org/wiki/Five_whys

I like to start **IMPROVEMENT** through Risk Management of the specific objective, considering strengths and opportunities to explore and weaknesses and threats to mitigate; all qualified in probability and impact.

Thus, action plans, responses to risks or contingencies emerge more easily, in this transition between Analysis and Improvement sections.

Think about the questions: "What makes it worse?" and "what makes it better?"; all with well-defined deadlines, responsible persons and situations.

I believe in **CONTROL** obtained through the initiatives of a dedicated Training Plan, preparing the results until your next review.

As we wanted to demonstrate, it really is a single sheet, well grouped, very visual, for each objective and highly personalized: a dynamic infographic!

Software solutions for OKRs

Systematizing processes will always be attractive!

So, understand: whenever there is a process, development or management, with well-defined activities and states, there will always be some associated software tool.

Because, in reality, most existing software solutions are just the automation of some process, with its built-in business rules: insert data, query data, update data and delete data ... it's hard to escape from that! (laughter)

The value is, obviously, more in the knowledge and mastery of the **process** than in the acquisition of the best electronic tool; but you can, of course, obtain gains in grip and agility through a good choice ... just like everything else in life.

Therefore, I considered recording, here, my brief experience of using applications dedicated to OKRs.

The key to success lies in not following so eagerly, immediately searching for links on the internet: you won't even know exactly what you're looking for or you won't be sure what you found...

When there are several alternatives at stake, it is desirable to establish a preliminary list of **criteria**, in compliance with truly initial expectations.

This avoids temptations or illusions!

These criteria will guide a quick qualitative comparison, in a very objective way. If you wish to follow a more quantitative comparison, you can establish a **scoring scale** for each criterion, differentiate weights (multipliers) between the criteria and count everything in a matrix of alternatives (rows) versus criteria (columns): that resulting in more points is usually the best choice!

Please note: it is a **Decision Management** method!

In my desired enumeration, I would list:

- allow more than one key result per objective;
- be translated into native language (language option);
- offer a free plan when using essential features;
- reconcile access via application on cell phone and website on computer;
- present a visually attractive dashboard.

And then I would move on, in a qualitative analysis only; without as much rigor or risks for a quantitative assessment.

Because there are, indeed, many, many options; on any search for terms similar to "best OKR tools" or "*OKR tools*".

In returned results, most of the solutions presented are usually discarded due to the lack of my native language Brazilian Portuguese.

Measurement and Communication

In this criterion, it doesn't matter how many directors or managers are fluent in English in the company; the most important thing is that the entire organization is involved in A Management By Objectives... and, without translation to Brazilian Portuguese, the desired broad adoption will not occur.

Other criteria that, surprisingly, eliminate potential candidates are the lack of a free plan when using essential functionalities and the reconciliation of access via an app on a cell phone and a website on a computer.

Many tools bring the perception of an abusive commercial approach (due to the obligation to provide a credit card before starting tests) or have a really expensive pricing policy (with a clear "*enterprise*" preference, for large companies, without as much appreciation of the concept applicable to "*small business*").

Many tools also only operate through their "*desktop*" solution, without the existence of a related "*mobile*" application. And, for OKRs, such agility is desired, in consulting objectives and updating key results: you are not always in front of the computer and the cell phone browser does not always provide comfortable viewing.

You will even find one or another solution that treats OKRs as a measurement of individual performance and competence, especially for "*feedback* communications[3]" and replacement of (outdated) "360-degree feedback[4]", from HR: it doesn't make any sense to me!

In terms of positive points, almost all alternatives have a good visually attractive "*dashboard*" and almost all have good adherence to the conceptual model of OKRs; naturally allowing more than one key result per objective.

I therefore end up following the choice of the world's majority, of the most robust and professional tools:

---

[3] https://en.wikipedia.org/wiki/Feedback
[4] https://en.wikipedia.org/wiki/360-degree_feedback

- "Quantive[5]",
- "Peoplebox[6]",
- "Tability[7]".

In addition to one or more Key Results promoting the objectives, numerically or by percentage, it is important to contain a record of "Initiatives", without direct influence on the advancement of the result, but as an important note and call to action.

Key Results are also readily allocated into interesting "timelines", almost always considering the predefined quarterly update of objectives and the year divided into four periods ("*Quarter 1*", "*Quarter 2*", "*Quarter 3*", "*Quarter 4*").

But what really "sways" me, with the possibility of considering the adoption of software for OKRs, is when there is the possibility of **automatic integration** with other corporate tools: here, in my analysis, lies the value of the return on investment when contracting a commercial solution.

Integrating an OKR tool into a broader portfolio of tools, with all components "talking to each other" and supporting the company's communication, is something bigger and more consistent.

So, in comparison and as we wanted to demonstrate, there are advantages and disadvantages: both being able to speed up what is trivial in implementation, and creating some dependence on programmed limitations... choose, without fear, your destiny!

Reminder: Hey, manager, what is your objective within your company?

* * *

---

[5] https://quantive.com/
[6] https://www.peoplebox.ai/
[7] https://www.tability.io/

Just an additional excerpt, still related to software solutions: why not work on your own, customized solution for OKRs, through **relational databases**?

After all, this topic is still on the rise and I can already see my next book: "The End of Excel and the Growth of Connected Database Applications"! ;-)

In examples to try:

- "Fibery"[8];
- "Airtable"[9];
- "Notion"[10];
- "ClickUp"[11];
- "Jira"[12];
- "Pipefy"[13].

Here, then, is a brief presentation of the topic **Object-Relational Mapping**, applied to OKRs.

An **Objective** is formed by:

- title,
- % progress and
- key results.

A **Key Result** is formed by:

- title,
- initial value,
- goal value,

---

[8] https://fibery.io/
[9] https://www.airtable.com/
[10] https://www.notion.so/pt-br/product
[11] https://clickup.com/
[12] https://www.atlassian.com/software/jira
[13] https://www.pipefy.com/pt-br/

- current value and
- % progress.

Remembering that an Objective can have 1 or more Key Results.

It is clear to understand just two necessary tables, and their respective attributes, incorporating simple mathematical formulas and enabling free viewing options for this data.

Goal Progress % = (KR1 Progress % + KR2 Progress % + KR3 Progress %) / 3

KR Progress % = (([Current Value] - [Initial Value]) / ([Goal Value] - [Initial Value])) * 100

- List and Numerical Progress of Objectives,
- Objectives Scoreboard Signage (green, "we deliverED"; yellow, "progress, but not ready"; red, "no progress"),
- List and Numerical Progress of Key Results,
- Bar Chart Overview of Key Results.

If desired, it is easy to extend the association of **Initiatives** to Key Results (a Key Result can have 1 or more Initiatives).

An **Initiative** being formed by:

- title,
- responsible person,
- creation date,
- last modification,
- status ("next", "in progress", "completed"),
- files and
- comments.

I really like monitoring and quantifying completed initiatives, both by key results and objectives: after all, it's what drives this entire structure!

Now, you can also create your own application! ;-)

To learn more, I suggest researching the term **"ORM"** (*"Object-Relational Mapping"*) and my personal reference on the subject, Scott Ambler[14].

...because freedom is always a good choice!

Communication

"You don't need to talk. I read a book in your eyes. But I'd be fine if I didn't know your name. I haven't seen you in a while. And do I still feel that desire? And just thinking that I have to stay here, still, soon the loneliness gives way; it doesn't take long for loneliness to give you its arm, for you to come in... There's no need to talk and there's no need to mix things up: I know things aren't always as they should be. But they could be. And they should be. But it might be easier to tell you this. Easier to tell you, this." – Suricato, "You don't need to talk", ("Não Precisa Falar" in Brazilian Portuguese).

The data is already there, collected.

The results of the analyzes also, from complementary points of view.

The progress towards the objectives then continues to be consolidated.

We know who the interested parties are and, therefore, we make these records available.

But is this enough to say that communication was successful?

Does the evaluation carried out guarantee that future decisions will remain consistent and will benefit?

Yes, everything can still go wrong! (astonished)

---

[14] https://scottambler.com/

After so much effort, we can still "die on the beach"... if we neglect this important final step, closing the proposed process.

And, like any cycle, what we intend, intentionally, is to begin from a starting point and end with a recurrence of that same starting point.

The starting point is collaboration: at the beginning, in the middle and back to the beginning.

As in the infographic that illustrates the cover of this book: starting from a good strategy, we will have better results, proportional to our commitment.

This is the baseline of the demonstrated content and this must be the alignment of our execution, from the beginning: involve everyone!

Recalling the development process adopted for this project ("Establish and maintain commitment", "Plan the measurement", "Execute the measurement" and "Evaluate the measurement and its communication"), we now just need to "close the circle" and start all over again.

Let's, then, return to the ceremony of a "Commitment to a Management By Objectives".

Right! Here, we carry out a regular ritual of a collective debate meeting on the Management By Objectives report... and conducted by the employees themselves!

Yes, excessive meetings should be avoided at all costs (laughs), but I know that this is a meeting desired and awaited by many: after all, these are the leaders at work!

As I write this book, I have this next appointment in 2 weeks and I already have collaborators allocated to present each objective: my role, as CEO, will only be to learn... wow!

Ok, I'm also going to give a good (inviting to the most resistant) coffee break... (laughs)

Central Idea: this is how an organization's culture of excellence is formed: alive and evolving!

The success

"I am not done changing. Out on the run, changing. I may be old and I may be young. But I am not done changing." – John Mayer, "Changing"

As we approach the conclusion, let's review and question our foundations a little more, in a *"checklist"* of adherence to our progress and success; below.

- Are the objectives very specific, restricted, or are they, desirably, comprehensive, considering both quantity and quality?
- Are the objectives really challenging, knowing that skills, motivation, self-efficacy and training will be promoted in achieving the goals?
- Do employees help to establish the defined goals, in participation and commitment, in an agile and multidirectional way?
- Are ethical behavior and psychological safety ensured, in organizational culture, leadership and controls, to achieve goals?
- Are final results, both performance and learning, expected and considered by the organization, in terms of the path, the trajectory, the experiments and the best version?
- Is there explicit executive sponsorship from the CEO and strong support from the company's senior management in its OKRs implementation program?
- Are teams prepared for the discipline of weekly check-ins ceremonies, cadence review meetings, and *"feedback"* and *"coaching"* sessions?
- Are you using OKRs, as a goal management system, just because Google also uses it?

Consider these questions so as not to underestimate the challenges and resistance, in addition to avoiding known mistakes and pitfalls along the way; thus strengthening its implementation.

PART VI A NEW VISION

Innovation

"I can see clearly now the rain is gone. I can see all obstacles in my way. Gone are the dark clouds that had me blind. It's gonna be a bright, bright sunshiny day. It's gonna be a bright, bright sunshiny day. Oh, yes I can make it now the pain is gone. All of the bad feelings have disappeared. Here is that rainbow I've been praying for. It's gonna be a bright, bright sunshiny day. look all around, there's nothing but blue skies. Look straight ahead, there's nothing but blue skies!" – Johnny Nash, "I Can See Clearly Now"

"**One Process** to rule them all, **One Process** to find them, **One Process** to bring them all..."

Paraphrasing quotes from J. R. R. Tolkien's work, in "The Lord of the Rings", I think I have found "the master ring", "the ring of Sauron", "the ring of power", "the One Ring", "My Precious": the **Process for Process Definition**!

Having this **meta process**, mapped to define any process, to review and optimize other processes, a beautiful reusable abstraction is achieved, based on a generic process that will instantiate all other real processes.

Look around you: it has always worked like this, and perhaps you haven't realized it yet...

Examples of agile methods[1], so in hype, "Scrum"[2], "Kanban"[3], "Lean"[4] they are just processes!

Indeed, I love Scrum, Kanban and Lean (no criticism, quite the opposite); but it is important to note that they are processes

---

[1] https://en.wikipedia.org/wiki/Agile_software_development
[2] https://en.wikipedia.org/wiki/Scrum
[3] https://en.wikipedia.org/wiki/Kanban
[4] https://en.wikipedia.org/wiki/Lean_manufacturing

contained and instantiated within a broad culture of **Management By Processes**, differing from each other only in terms of the approaches to their activities.

Therefore, I understand a certified professional in these examples as a valuable **Process Specialist** (in a dedicated, specific process). While I understand a certified professional in Business Processes as a creative **Process Architect** (for any new process).

Still thinking about "The Lord of the Rings", I think I've already been to "Land of Mordor"[5] (nervous laughter from my own experiences) and I believe it is fundamental such clarifications, where does the **innovation** Part VI comes from: people have called everything "agile methods", when they should just call them "processes"... because, obviously, not every process meets the specific characteristics of agility!

Therefore, please be very careful when reading other references to the **Management By Objectives** also called an "agile method": it doesn't make any sense and only demonstrates a complete lack of understanding of all associated scenarios. If someone tells me that OKRs represent an agile method, I immediately distrust that content source.

Central Idea: Ok, our Management By Objectives has its own development process and makes up our personalized understanding of Integrated Management, but many methods have similarities because, in common, they are processes, not because they are always agile!

---

[5]https://en.wikipedia.org/wiki/Mordor

Culture

"Sometimes in our lives. We all have pain. We all have sorrow. But if we are wise. We know that there's always tomorrow. Lean on me. When you're not strong. And I'll be your friend. I'll help you carry on... For it won't be long. Till I'm gonna need somebody to lean on."
– Bill Withers, "Lean On Me"

From everything we've already talked about and learned, doesn't it still seem like it will be difficult to implement and maintain the full scope of a Management By Objectives throughout the organization, without exceptions?

From the "1 on 1" meetings[1], from the "CFRs" (conversation, feedback, recognition), we then extended "Management By Objectives Committees", increasing the cardinality of relationships and performance gains.

But the OKRs revolution really integrates and "brings to light" other necessary and much more structural changes... that we don't always have the courage to face (or write)!

How does your **formal and traditional organization chart** work around **innovative and challenging key results**?

Don't you think there are inconsistencies between their different forms and functions? Don't you think that key results only tolerate the classic organizational chart, but don't complement synergy?

Well: strengthening hierarchical levels may not be too disruptive, but it certainly does not bring additional benefits to the new system.

My innovation: throw away, as soon as possible, the custom of the old model, outside of the current situation presented; In time, it will be out of use and you will have anticipated superior performance!

---

[1] https://en.everybodywiki.com/1_on_1_meeting

How? In a new **physical-functional organization chart**.

"Physical" because it is occupied by people, in explicit and broad attribution of individual responsibilities: everyone is named and is potentially valued... making the complete origin of formation of the "legal person" clearer.

"Functional" because it is more dynamic, more fluid in its vertical boundaries, more oriented towards meritocracy[2] and collaboration... without losing the definition and expected practices of each scope of action.

Reinforcing what has already been presented in previous chapters, I continue with the definition of 4 internal organizational roles:

• **"Process Owners"**: the basic and fundamental unit of adherence to any work carried out, at a higher level (they all matter).

• **"Service Owners"**: a democratic interface, transition between processes and operations, strengthening the dissemination of calm, organized, managed and productive environments;

• **"Operations Owners"**: senior management, the trusted network of experts, in strategic business support;

• **"Product Owners"**: the board of partners, directors and executive leaders, in a new look at the organization when managing a product;

This way, everything contributes to less value being given to the formalizations, limitations and competitions of "assistants", "analysts", "managers" or "directors"...

And the delivery of **key results** takes place over and above the accounting signature of the Work Card: although respect for the second is maintained, we try and promote the first more!

* * *

[2] https://en.wikipedia.org/wiki/Meritocracy

Culture

Let's talk a little more about the beauty of the processes!

There are processes in everything I see... (laughs)

Tell me an agile method[3] and I'll give you back the generic mapping of this process.

But without the exaggeration of the evangelists on duty, without limiting ourselves to the universe of software development or tying ourselves into a single industry: we will continue adapting our activities and nomenclatures to the scope of projects, services and products... it's time to take risks and allow ourselves!

Ok, we know that there is no single, perfect "Silver Bullet"[4], capable of killing "werewolf, witch or any other monster"; but there is, indeed, the possibility of combining methods in an extended scope: A Agile Management By Objectives!

From the previous sections, our OKRs and KPIs now incorporate agility characteristics, in a new way of working.

Every day, gather your team around a brief 15-minute ceremony, to align what results we advanced the previous day, what the advances will be today and what impediments are making the results harder: a **Daily Meeting** of Key Results... and stop tripping over those small stones along the way!

Maintaining these daily values of **pace, commitment and adaptation**, continue evolving your next action plans into Prioritized Lists ("*backlogs*") of Continuous Improvement and Management of Events, Incidents and Problems: this way, you will achieve guaranteed maturity and capacity.

And where do you and your team want to be, or get to, tomorrow, next week or at the end of the month? This period, widely known as "*Sprint*", is nothing more than planning goals for A Management By Objectives; and may also be a favorable increase in the formation of leadership.

---

[3]https://en.wikipedia.org/wiki/Agile_software_development
[4]https://en.wikipedia.org/wiki/Silver_bullet

Within the recurrence of these periods of "*sprints*", maintain a regular **review** of your development processes, based on existing acceptance and identification criteria for the process movements carried out: such "contracts" are what make the activities and the results as completed, that is, they are your "**Definitions of Ready**".

In a retrospective look (bimonthly or quarterly), formalize your percentages of completion of key results, updating an executive scoreboard: your Management By Objectives Performance Indicator Measurement Report.

The new physical-functional organization chart ("product owners", "operations owners", "service owners", "process owners") will already bring you the necessary harmony to control these work products: in **papers** , **ceremonies** and **artifacts** integrated into processes and objectives!

Note 1: all terms marked in bold above are fundamental characteristics of Scrum[5] Agile Development, and can be analyzed, comparatively, under the broader perspective of Management By Processes and A Management By Objectives.

Note 2: although the innovative association between Agile Management, Management By Processes and Management By Objectives is proven here, we are still only dealing with an approximation, not a fusion of identities (or entities). ;-)

In any case, go further: you were not born to just be "Scrum Master"[6]! (laughter)

---

[5] https://en.wikipedia.org/wiki/Scrum_(software_development)
[6] https://wiki.ncrcolibri.com.br/display/scrum/Scrum+Master

A Life for Goals

"From all my past, good and bad memories. I want to live my present! And remember everything later... In this passing life, I am me, you are you. That's what pleases me most, that's what makes me say: that I see flowers in you! That I see flowers in you! That I see flowers in you!" – Ira, "Flowers In You" ("Flores Em Você" in Portuguese)

"Everything is a process: life and business are processes that present variations, which, however natural and expected, must be reduced": I loved this phrase, which I received during the critical reading stage of the first edition of this book; made especially by Graciléa Rodrigues[1], from Monitore Negócios[2]!

In this section, I seek to illuminate this transition: from business goals to life goals!

Obviously, this text is not a self-help chapter: it will not surprise you to realize that it is, more, a self-learning by the author, a case report of writing the book itself; because the more I teach, the more I learn.

At the end of this knowledge process, I accepted that there is the possibility of working on professional goals and personal goals, in full synergy:

- in a **responsible**, but **light** manner;
- **continuously**, but **without anxiety**;
- in a **complete** way, in choosing **priorities**;
- in a **collaborative** way, accepting new **ideas**;
- in an **adaptive** way, embracing **changes**.

---
[1] https://www.linkedin.com/in/gracilearodrigues-mne/
[2] @monitorenegocios

Note, in evidence: I actually needed to postpone the launch of a first version, to support my daughter in her school exams and to support my company in its external audits; all concentrated simultaneously in the same year.

But everything is still going well: the monitoring and evolution of the **objectives** established and their **key results** defined, prioritized and documented continues; in grateful balance!

It's a new perception of **prosperity**: everything is managed and everything is managed for happiness!

Therefore, both for work and for family, a better organization of objectives is possible (and very interesting), in complete terms from the perspectives of a BSC ("*Balanced Scorecard*"): • objectives from a financial perspective, • objectives from customers' perspective, • objectives from the perspective of internal processes and • objectives from a learning and growth perspective.

Similarly, it is easy to establish professional and personal OKRs, using the same writing format already studied.

But, if desired, just for monitoring personal objectives, it would be worth a huge simplification of the wording, in some examples below, which we will not consider a sin (laughs), for now.

- "By [date], add [amount] to financial reserves."
- "By [date], add [amount], in commercial sales".
- "By [date], add [amount], in pages read".
- "By [date], add [amount], in written pages".
- "By [date], add [amount], in hobby hours."
- "By [date], add [amount], in language classes".

And always maintaining the insistent and resilient practice of **initiatives**, promoting the evolution of key results.

In your Life Management by Objectives, stay focused, get rid of distractions and don't fool yourself!

WHAT LEFT TO BE SAID?

About me and where we meet

It is already customary, in my books, to leave personal considerations at the end! ;-)

It makes more sense to me: start, as quickly as possible, with what matters; and then conclude together whether expectations were met.

I wrote both editions of this book in simultaneous real implementations: the first, as a "Minimum Viable Product"[1], both for the company and for readers; the second, as a complete and refined product. The study, whether essential or advanced, always evolved into practice the following week; and vice versa!

This model, of only recording what had already been tested and accepting new learning while teaching the previous study, perhaps delayed all these versions and publications significantly; but I hope to have had results in more evident truth, in the words of each chapter.

For many, the simple literal translation of the theme "OKRs", to Objectives and Key Results, seems to be enough; and it is no surprise that, in this absurd simplification, everything goes wrong and continues to be superficial propaganda, of concepts and implementation.

When someone told me "oh, Objectives and Key Results, I already understand everything", I noticed a greater and growing need for extended writing on the subject. (laughter)

Even without the intention of registering my work, it seemed to me, while studying, that there were only two scenarios: 1) John

---

[1] https://en.wikipedia.org/wiki/Minimum_viable_product

Doerr's book and 2) all other publications, in copies or shallow translations of this reference book (they don't even mention the book by Andrew Grove).

I loved John Doerr's book! But I still found it incomplete, for my reality. And, as I was unable to clarify all my doubts, in the additional readings, I accepted the challenge of starting my own essay... here completed to the public's liking and presented to you!

* * *

It's also a little strange to end a book without having, in the slightest way, introduced myself...

Therefore, here is a brief mini CV, respectfully and quickly.

I'm Maria Luíza's father, Flávia's husband, founder of the CPBiz business school, CEO of Fonte Patologia Oncológica and I'm still trying to learn to play the electric guitar.

I have always been an **engineer** and I have always been linked to **processes** and **software**.

I graduated as a **Chemical Engineer** from the Federal University of Rio de Janeiro[2] and began my professional career developing automatic control **software** for industrial **processes** manufacturing, as **Automation Engineer**, for 10 years. I acquired several professional certifications in computer programming and migrated to **Software Engineer** of business **processes**, for 5 years. I completed an MBA in Project Management, from Instituto Infnet[3] (where I also worked as a brief teacher, in extension courses), I sought new professional certifications in * *processes* * and moved on to business consultancy. I also recently became a "Certified OKR Practitioner"[4] (C-OKRP), in a wonderful training offered by OKR International[5].

[2] https://ufrj.br/
[3] https://www.infnet.edu.br/infnet/instituto/
[4] https://okrinternational.com/certified-okr-practitioner-okr-coach-certification/
[5] https://okrinternational.com/

From there, I add my previous experience as an industrial process automation engineer and software development in information technology to the current executive direction of a medical laboratory, as health business manager. I have accumulated management experience and professional license certifications in corporate governance, business development, general management and technology. I maintain my work through strategic alignment, formation of high-performance teams and a focus on quality. On a daily basis, I am an agent of organizational change, with negotiation skills, creative strategies and the ability to regroup, reorganize and deliver results. My books also add value to the company's brand as an author.

Our "meeting place", to share "all that physically exists, the entirety of space and time and all forms of matter, including all planets, stars, galaxies and the components of intergalactic space" by author, trainer and consultant it will, for now, be via **LinkedIn** (https://www.linkedin.com/in/cpbiz/): everything still points there and most of the useful information continues there!

Soon, I intend to organize a new professional profile space on **Teachable**, on my own domain www.claudiopires.biz, where my books, translations, consultancy notebooks, audiobooks, online courses and our community of practice will be gathered.

On **Instagram** @claudiopires.biz, I communicate consolidated advances and upcoming plans, in the best "a coffee, a cake, a book and a solution" style! ;-)

I also reinforce my full availability for direct contacts: send me an **e-mail** to contato@claudiopires.biz.

Having come this far, I just have to thank you for all your time and attention and wish you a great practice!

In a sincere and cordial manner, I remain at your disposal and thank you very much!

About my books and the Management in Practice series

With each copy, the order in which it is written or read matters less: the publication of a new book complements and advances the same series, which always brings together the learning of management in practice.

It is a proposal for continuous improvement, risks and opportunities, strategy and performance assessment: both for the author and for the reader.

We start from any volume or topic of interest and, little by little, we create our own path: incorporating the lessons learned and evolving towards new challenges.

Currently, there are 3 titles:

• "Management By Processes in Practice: where to start your business processes culture" – book 1 of the Management in Practice series.

• "Business Management: MBA in Practice; how to organize your company in 100 days" – book 2 of the Management in Practice series.

• "A Management By Objectives: OKR and BPM Together in Practice; the strategic management of your business processes" – book 3 of the Management in Practice series.

All books are sold concentrated (not exclusive) on Amazon[1]: in Kindle eBook and printed version formats. I have also expanded

---

[1] https://www.amazon.com/kindle-dbs/entity/author?asin=B001JY6EFG

publications in audio format (audiobooks on different platforms) and in translations into other languages (preferably Spanish and English). And, for each book, I plan a respective course (distance learning, in-person teaching, in-company training, webinar, consultancy and mentoring): get in touch.

This series represents independent publications, without the involvement of an established publisher: from the term "*indie author*". Thus, all costs, direct or indirect, are borne by the author himself.

It's not about the inability to find a publisher who is interested and makes investments; It's worth more as a choice for editorial freedom: I fully publish my truth.

Starting, then, from the principle of writing with my own style and respectful grammatical adherence, the biggest problem with self-published books lies in the fact that these books are rarer to obtain recognition and are more difficult to find.

Therefore, **your comment makes all the difference**: if you can, return your evaluation and your impressions, freely disseminated through social networks and reading platforms (mainly on **Amazon**).

This is a **great revolution to value!**

And as an author, I want my books to also add value to your company's brand, in professional and business development.

Thank you!

www.ingramcontent.com/pod-product-compliance
Lightning Source LLC
Chambersburg PA
CBHW072052230526